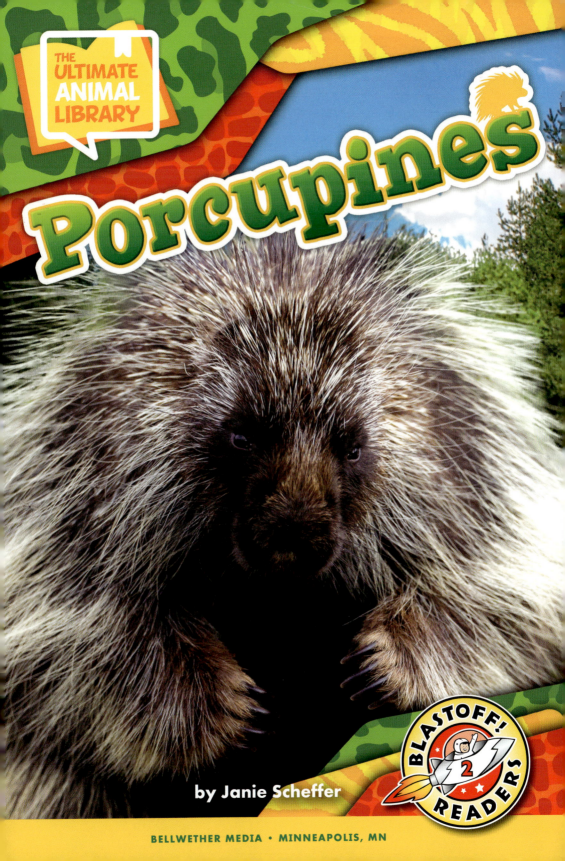

THE ULTIMATE ANIMAL LIBRARY

Porcupines

by Janie Scheffer

BLASTOFF! READERS 2

BELLWETHER MEDIA • MINNEAPOLIS, MN

Blastoff! Readers are carefully developed by literacy experts to build reading stamina and move students toward fluency by combining standards-based content with developmentally appropriate text.

LEVELS

Level 1 provides the most support through repetition of high-frequency words, light text, predictable sentence patterns, and strong visual support.

Level 2 offers early readers a bit more challenge through varied sentences, increased text load, and text-supportive special features.

Level 3 advances early-fluent readers toward fluency through increased text load, less reliance on photos, advancing concepts, longer sentences, and more complex special features.

★ **Blastoff! Universe**

Reading Level

Grade K

Grades 1–3

Grade 4

This edition first published in 2026 by Bellwether Media, Inc.

No part of this publication may be reproduced in whole or in part without written permission of the publisher. For information regarding permission, write to Bellwether Media, Inc., Attention: Permissions Department, 3500 American Blvd W, Suite 150, Bloomington, MN 55431.

Library of Congress Cataloging-in-Publication Data

LC record for Porcupines available at: https://lccn.loc.gov/2025003954

Text copyright © 2026 by Bellwether Media, Inc. BLASTOFF! READERS and associated logos are trademarks and/or registered trademarks of Bellwether Media, Inc. Bellwether Media is a division of FlutterBee Education Group.

Editor: Elizabeth Neuenfeldt   Series Designer: Veah Demmin

Printed in the United States of America, North Mankato, MN.

Table of Contents

What Are Porcupines?	4
Climbers and Swimmers!	12
Growing Up	18
Glossary	22
To Learn More	23
Index	24

What Are Porcupines?

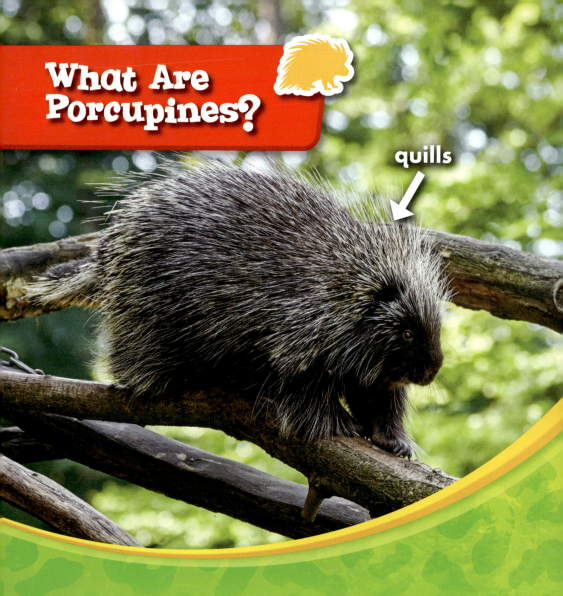

quills

Porcupines are large **rodents**. They are best known for their **quills**. These **mammals** live around the world. Many live in North America.

North American Porcupine Report

Range

range = 🟥

Status in the Wild

least concern

Habitats

forests

grasslands

shrublands

Porcupines have round bodies. Their heads and ears are small.

ear

Their fur is mostly dark brown or black. About 30,000 white quills are mixed in.

Quills have very sharp tips. They keep porcupines safe.

When **predators** attack, the quills come off. They get stuck on predators!

predator

quills

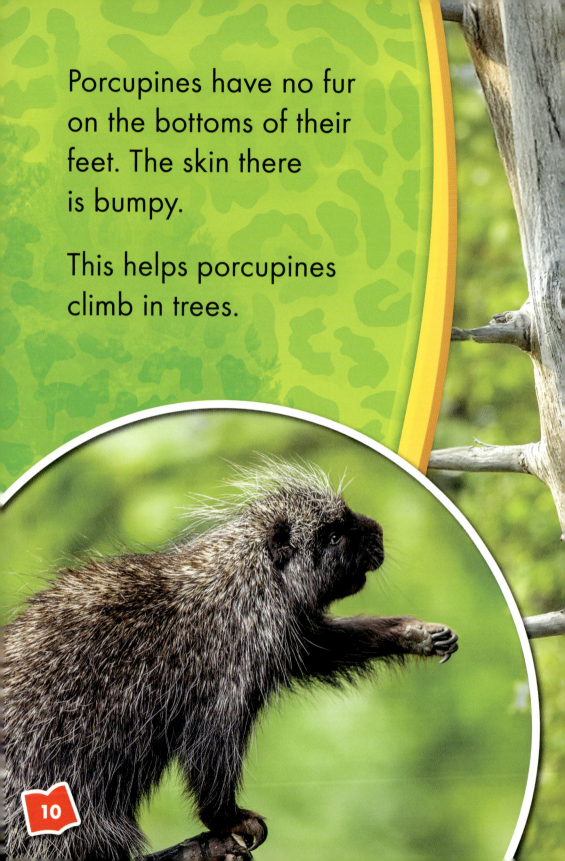

Porcupines have no fur on the bottoms of their feet. The skin there is bumpy.

This helps porcupines climb in trees.

Climbers and Swimmers!

Porcupines mostly live in forests. They usually live alone.

They may rest together in **dens** during winter. They make dens in trees and logs.

den

Porcupines are strong swimmers and climbers. This helps them find food in all seasons.

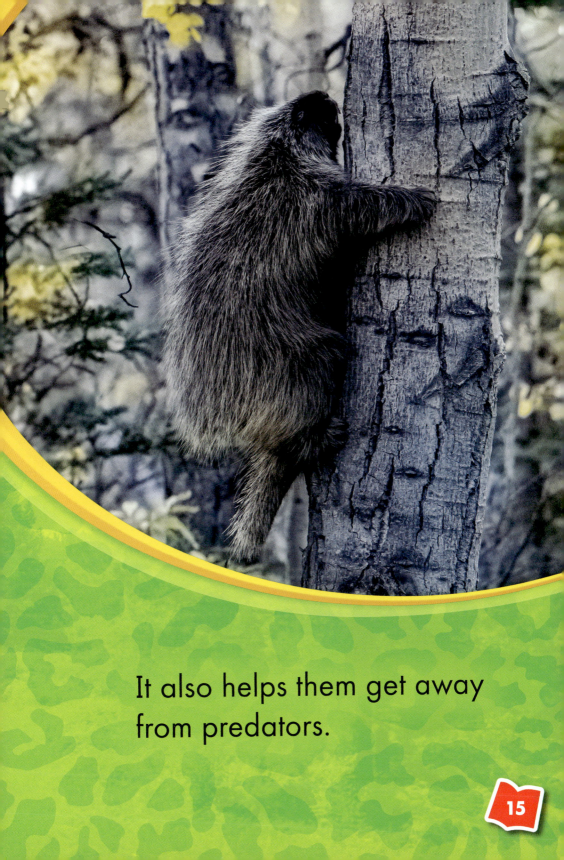

It also helps them get away from predators.

Porcupines are mostly **nocturnal**. They find food at night.

They are **herbivores**. They eat twigs and bark. They eat plants and fruits, too.

Growing Up

Male porcupines call and dance to find **mates**. Later, females give birth to one **porcupette**.

Porcupettes are born with soft quills. The quills harden an hour later.

porcupette

A few weeks after birth, porcupettes can eat plants. At about six months old, they leave their mothers.

These rodents can live for around 20 years!

Life of a Porcupine

Name of Babies

 porcupettes

Number of Babies

 1

Time Spent with Mom

 about 6 months

Life Span

 around 20 years

Glossary

dens—sheltered places

herbivores—animals that only eat plants

mammals—warm-blooded animals that have backbones and feed their young milk

mates—partners

nocturnal—active at night

porcupette—a baby porcupine

predators—animals that hunt other animals for food

quills—sharp spines with unfilled space on the inside

rodents—small animals that gnaw on their food

To Learn More

AT THE LIBRARY

Bahn, Christopher. *Porcupines*. Mankato, Minn.: Creative Education, 2025.

Rex, Ruby. *Deadly Quills: Gross Porcupines*. Minneapolis, Minn.: Bearport Publishing Company, 2023.

Rice, Jamie. *Hedgehog or Porcupine?* Minneapolis, Minn.: Jump!, 2023.

ON THE WEB

FACTSURFER

Factsurfer.com gives you a safe, fun way to find more information.

1. Go to www.factsurfer.com.

2. Enter "porcupines" into the search box and click 🔍.

3. Select your book cover to see a list of related content.

Index

bodies, 6
climb, 10, 14
colors, 7
dens, 13
ears, 6
feet, 10
females, 18
food, 14, 16, 17, 20
forests, 12
fur, 7, 10
heads, 6
herbivores, 17
life of a porcupine, 21
logs, 13
males, 18
mammals, 4
mates, 18
mothers, 20
night, 16
nocturnal, 16
North America, 4

porcupette, 18, 19, 20
predators, 9, 15
quills, 4, 7, 8, 9, 18
range, 4, 5
rodents, 4, 21
size, 4, 6
skin, 10
spot a porcupine, 11
status, 5
swimmers, 14
trees, 10, 13
winter, 13

The images in this book are reproduced through the courtesy of: Jukka Jantunen, cover (porcupine), p. 14; Mahirov9, cover background, interior background; Kozyreva Elena, cover (porcupine icon); Eric Isselée, pp. 3, 11, 23; Jens, p. 4; imphilip, p. 6; Susan, pp. 7, 12; htrnr, p. 8; Design Pics Ince/ Alamy, p. 9; Nick Fox, p. 10; outdoorsman, pp. 10-11; Nature Picture Library/ Alamy, p. 13; Pascale Gueret, p. 15; geoffkuchera, pp. 16-17, 17 (fishers), 18-19; Sarka, p. 17 (twigs and bark); Erni, p. 17 (lynx); Andrey Zyk, p. 17 (plants); Hanjo Hellmann, p. 17 (porcupine); John Yunker, p. 17 (coyotes); Kaja, p. 17 (fruits); dssimages, p. 18; Designpics, p. 20; hkuchera, p. 21.